Human Rights

AS A CHILD

HUMAN RIGHTS

AS A CHILD

Safeguarding Children's Rights

written by

Elizabeth Dale Schetina

Rourke Corporation, Inc.
Vero Beach, Florida 32964

Cover design: David Hundley

∞ The paper used in this book conforms to the American
National Standard for Permanence of Paper for Printed
Library Materials, Z39.48-1984.

Library of Congress Cataloging-in-Publication Data
Schetina, Elizabeth Dale, 1961-
    As a child: safeguarding children's rights / by Elizabeth
Dale Schetina.
        p.   cm. — (Human rights)
    Includes bibliographical references and index.
    Summary: Defines children's rights and discusses them
in the context of the home, school, workplace, and
elsewhere.
    ISBN 0-86593-176-3 (alk. paper)
    1.   Children — Legal   status,   laws,   etc. — United
States — Juvenile   literature.   2.   Children's   rights —
United   States — Juvenile   literature.   [1.   Children's
rights.]   I. Title.   II. Series: Human rights (Vero
Beach, Fla.)
KF479.Z9S495   1992   92-9748
346.7301'35 — dc20   CIP
[347.306135]   AC

PRINTED IN THE UNITED STATES OF AMERICA

Contents

Human Rights

AS A CHILD

Chapter One

What Are Children's Rights?

All people have rights called human rights. Some human rights are moral rights and some human rights are legal rights. Moral rights include the right to follow one's own beliefs, to live in peace, and to be happy. Legal rights include the right to free public education, to vote, and to work in safe and healthy conditions. Some moral rights have been made into legal rights. For example, in the Constitution of the United States, the Bill of Rights guarantees that all citizens have the right to practice any religion, to live where they choose, and to speak their minds freely.

Both adults and children have human rights. However, children do not have the same moral or legal rights as adults. Children's rights are different from those of adults because children are different from adults. Children need protection; they need to learn about the world and have a chance to grow.

The United Nations has considered children's need for unique rights to protect them. The U.N. General Assembly adopted a Declaration of the Rights of the Child in 1959. That declaration listed the moral and legal rights that children in all countries deserve:

> The child shall enjoy special protection and shall be given opportunities and facilities to enable him to develop in a healthy and normal manner, in conditions of freedom and dignity. . . .

It contained provisions stating that children shall have the benefits of social security, adequate nutrition, decent housing, love and understanding, moral and material security, free and compulsory education, full opportunity for play and recreation, and an atmosphere of tolerance, friendship, peace, and brotherhood.

In 1989, the U.N. Convention on the Rights of the Child updated the Declaration of the Rights of the Child. The 1989 declaration contains most of the same rights as the earlier declaration and adds that children need special safeguards, that the best environment for the child is the family, and that governments should be committed to helping children. The 1989 declaration also gives children the right to participate in the culture of their society.

Children's Rights in North America

Society, the courts, and lawmakers have been concerned about children's rights since the beginning of the twentieth century. As a result, children's legal rights are very different from those of adults. Some people may think that children and teenagers have an easy life, with too much freedom — that they have "got it made." Young people, on the other hand, may think that there are many things in their lives that are not fair and that they lack the freedom and power that adults have. In fact, children enjoy rights and protections that adults do not have, but they lack some rights and freedoms that adults enjoy.

First, children have many rights that others do not have. Children have the right to a free public education. They have the right to be cared for and supported by someone else. Children do not have to work before a certain age, and, when they do work, they have the right to work only a certain

Percentage of Children in the U.S. Population

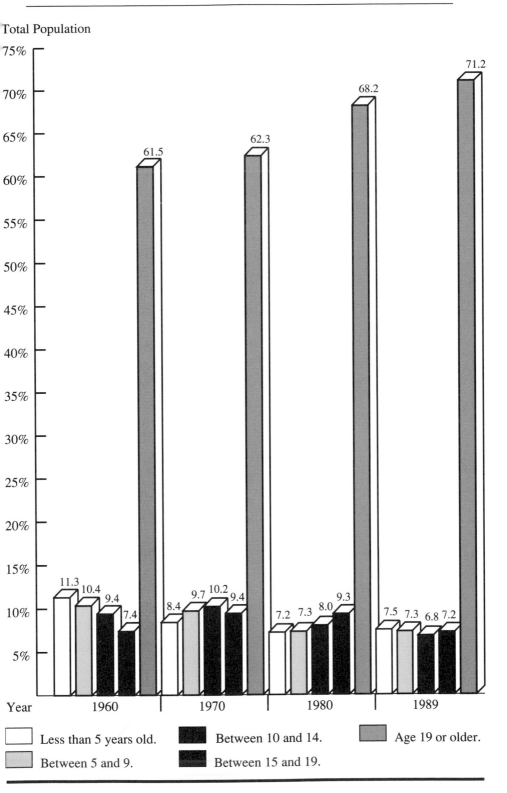

Total Population

| Year | 1960 | 1970 | 1980 | 1989 |

Legend:
- Less than 5 years old.
- Between 5 and 9.
- Between 10 and 14.
- Between 15 and 19.
- Age 19 or older.

1960: 11.3, 10.4, 9.4, 7.4, 61.5
1970: 8.4, 9.7, 10.2, 9.4, 62.3
1980: 7.2, 7.3, 8.0, 9.3, 68.2
1989: 7.5, 7.3, 6.8, 7.2, 71.2

number of hours and at certain jobs. The law also protects children in special ways. Children have the right to be protected from abuse and neglect, and the government tries to ensure that children enjoy a minimum standard of care and have a proper home, food, and medical attention. Children have other unique protections not related to their care. For example, a child cannot be held to a contract that he or she has made with an adult or with another child.

However, children lack some of the legal rights and freedoms that adults can exercise. Children are not free to leave school, cannot vote, cannot drive, and cannot get married without their parents' permission. Children are not free to leave their homes until they are eighteen or twenty-one years of age, depending on where they live. Children can be forced to obey parents and teachers, and they can be physically punished if they do not obey. Also, children cannot keep the money they earn, unless their parents allow them to, and they cannot make a will. So, while children are protected and have special legal rights that adults do not have, they also lack rights and freedoms guaranteed to other citizens. Children's legal status is clearly very different from that of adults.

Who Has This Special Legal Status?

When children's rights are discussed, it is important to know exactly who "children" are. What group of people has this special legal status?

Children's rights apply to all *minors*. Minors are those people who are under a certain age, called the *age of majority*, and who are under the control of their parents or guardians. Minors are said to be "below the age of majority." The age of majority varies from state to state, but it is usually eighteen years of age. In some states the age of majority is nineteen years of age, and in others it is twenty-one years of age. Once a minor reaches the age of majority, he or she is considered an

the right of the child

to education

to science

The child of today is the man of tomorrow. Unesco builds for the future. The rights of the child have been proclaimed by the United Nations. In its daily action, Unesco gives these rights meaning.

to culture

The child has a right to education. Education must be free and compulsory. The child's interests must guide those responsible for his education. Scientific knowledge grows with the child. He must benefit from its advantages now. Later on he will be able to contribute to its advancement. The child is wrapped around by his people's culture. From his first childish words to his last breath, each individual adds to the culture of the whole of mankind. Through it, he reaches the universal. The child will talk and listen, learn to express himself and to understand what others are saying. He will construct the immense network of communication which will link together, without distraction and without discrimination, all the men and women of the twenty-first century.

to communication

unesco

Children's need for special rights has been recognized by the United Nations. (Library of Congress)

adult and is no longer controlled by parents or guardians. Minors below the age of majority are those who have what is called "children's rights."

It is possible for a child or teenager who is below the age of majority to become *emancipated*. If a minor is emancipated, he or she no longer has the legal status of a minor. An emancipated minor loses the protection and special status guaranteed by children's rights and instead has the legal rights of an adult. There are different ways minors can be emancipated, and these will be considered later in this book.

It is also possible for a minor to be above the age of majority for some purposes and still be below the age of majority for other purposes. For example, a minor may be able to obtain birth control after the age of fourteen, may be able to leave school at sixteen, yet may be required to live with parents, obey them, and give them any money she earns until the age of eighteen. In most states, however, a minor assumes all the rights and responsibilities of an adult after turning eighteen.

Chapter Two

Why Are Children's Rights Different?

Children are at a disadvantage in the adult world because they are physically and socially different from adults. Babies and young children cannot take care of themselves, so they are dependent on adults. Children are physically smaller than adults, making it easy for an adult to abuse them and making it difficult for them to function in the adult world, where everything is too big for them. Children have not learned what is dangerous and how to protect themselves. They do not know how to meet their own needs, and they may not fully understand what their needs are.

Children are also at risk of being exploited or abused because they do not have a voice in society. For example, they cannot vote. Finally, children are taught to obey and respect authority figures. Children learn that they must do what an adult tells them to do. Some adults take advantage of this power and harm children.

Abuses of Children in History

Even though physical and social differences have always made children vulnerable to abuse by adults, children have not always been protected. Two children in the late nineteenth

Child abuse is not new, as "Italian Boys in New York — Tortures of the Training Room," 1873, shows. (Library of Congress)

century helped show society that children need special rights and protections.

In the winter of 1869, in Illinois, Samuel Fletcher, Jr., was locked by his father and stepmother in a cold, damp cellar. Samuel, who was blind, managed to escape. When found, he was covered with lice. The town authorities sued Samuel's parents, and the court found them guilty of mistreating their son; his parents were fined. The judge said, "It would be monstrous to hold that under the pretense of sustaining parental authority, children must be left, without the protection of the law, at the mercy of depraved men or women, with liberty to inflict any species of barbarity short of the actual taking of life." The judge believed that parents should not be allowed to hurt their children just because they are their parents.

In 1874, a New York social worker tried to help an abused, seriously ill child, Mary Ellen. While visiting a tenement house, the social worker learned about the young girl, who had been beaten by her stepmother. Mary Ellen had been chained to her bed and fed only bread and water. However, the social worker found that there was no law making it illegal to abuse a child. The social worker turned to the Society for the Prevention of Cruelty to Animals (SPCA) and persuaded that organization to prosecute Mary Ellen's parents for mistreating a member of the animal species, a human child. The SPCA brought Mary Ellen's parents to court, and she was removed from their custody. They were found guilty and were sentenced to imprisonment in the penitentiary. Because of Mary Ellen, the New York Society for the Prevention of Cruelty to Children was founded in 1875.

The cases of Samuel Fletcher and Mary Ellen helped create laws to protect children against abuse and neglect. Laws to protect children were also needed to solve the problem of child labor. After the Civil War, when huge industrialized factories began to produce the nation's goods, many children were working in factories. Many immigrant families came to the United States and settled in eastern cities. They had a very hard time making a living, and many put their children to work in the factories. Outside the cities, children worked in mines or in fields as farm laborers. Children as young as four worked in factories or picked cotton. Children who toiled in mills, fields, and mines had an extremely hard life. Many states had laws that limited the number of hours that children could work or required children to attend school instead of working, but these laws were not enforced.

Protections for Children

Around the time that Samuel Fletcher and Mary Ellen were rescued from their abusive parents, society's attitude toward child labor began to change, and the working child began to be seen as a victim who was abused by the system. Hearing about children like Samuel Fletcher and Mary Ellen, and responding to the child labor problem, a number of people began a movement for reform. The reformers were social workers, teachers, members of the clergy, and others who wanted to improve the lives of many disadvantaged groups. Reformers wanted the government to establish guidelines for protecting children. They realized that some parents did not fulfill their duties toward their children and that many adults exploited children.

Some reformers wanted the government to assume all of the duties of parents and to have the government take care of all children. Other reformers wanted to help the entire family and believed that children would be better off if their parents were taught how to take good care of their own children at home. All the reformers, however, wanted the government to assume some responsibility for the welfare of children. Finally, Congress established the Children's Bureau in 1912. Children

Children require special protections before they become adults. (Martin Rogers/Uniphoto)

now had a government agency that worked to help and protect them. The Children's Bureau eventually became part of the Department of Health and Human Services.

The government assumed the responsibility for assisting parents in fulfilling their duties toward their children and for protecting children from parents who failed to fulfill their duties to their children. This government responsibility is called "protective paternalism," and it means that the government (usually the state government) protects the child as a parent would. Legally, this is called *parens patriae*. Under this system, the state has the right to act in the role of the parent, especially when the parent of a child has failed to do so or when the child has broken the law. Protective paternalism has expanded to the public school system, so that the school is said to be acting *in loco parentis*, or "in place of the parent," in such matters as discipline and punishment.

Chapter Three

Rights at Home

Most children and teenagers live in a home with family members, and most live with at least one parent or adult guardian. Parents care for their children out of love and a sense of duty. Children and teenagers stay with their families and contribute to family life for the same reasons. However, both parents and children have many specific legal duties and responsibilities to each other.

Parents' Duties to Children

Parents are required by law to support, protect, educate, and control their children. These duties were given to parents by different United States Supreme Court decisions and by decisions of different state supreme courts. By the same token, children have the right to be supported, protected, educated, and controlled by their parents. Children have these rights even if their parents have never been married and even if their parents are divorced or separated. Children also have these rights if they are in the custody of a guardian who is not a parent. If a minor becomes a parent, he or she has these same duties to his or her child.

First, parents are required to *support* their children. They must provide their children with the "necessaries" of life: food, clothing, and shelter. Parents must provide enough food, clothing, and shelter to keep their children healthy and well. However, it is the parents who decide what food, clothing, and shelter their children will have. What is provided does not have to be the best available or even the best the parents can afford, but it must be enough to keep the child healthy. A parent is not obligated to buy a child a new jacket for winter; it is sufficient for the parent to give the child a hand-me-down or handmade jacket, even if the child really wants a new jacket and hates the jacket offered. If the parents want to move to another state or to an apartment from a house, the child must go along too. If parents want another adult to care for their child, their child must live with that adult, although the parents retain their duties to their child. If parents have difficulty meeting their obligations to support their children, federal and state programs can help them. These programs try to ensure that all children enjoy the same minimum standard of care, by giving parents direct payments or food vouchers or supplements to help them support their children.

Next, parents must *protect* their children. This duty requires parents to safeguard the health, safety, and morals of their children. Parents are required to provide their children with sufficient medical care. A very sick child must see a doctor, even if the parents have religious beliefs that require them to try to heal a sick child by prayer instead. The duty to protect also requires parents to keep their children safe from people or things that may injure or hurt them. For example, a parent would be failing in his duty to protect if he let his child play with a loaded gun or in the winter snow in a swimsuit, or if he let another adult (including the child's other parent) abuse his child. Finally, the duty to protect gives parents the job of safeguarding their children's morals. Parents must prevent others from encouraging their children to act immorally, and cannot themselves encourage such behavior. In protecting a child's morals, the parent can decide what movies a child may see and whether the child must attend religious services.

Third, the law requires parents to *educate* their children. In most cases, parents send their children to public school. A

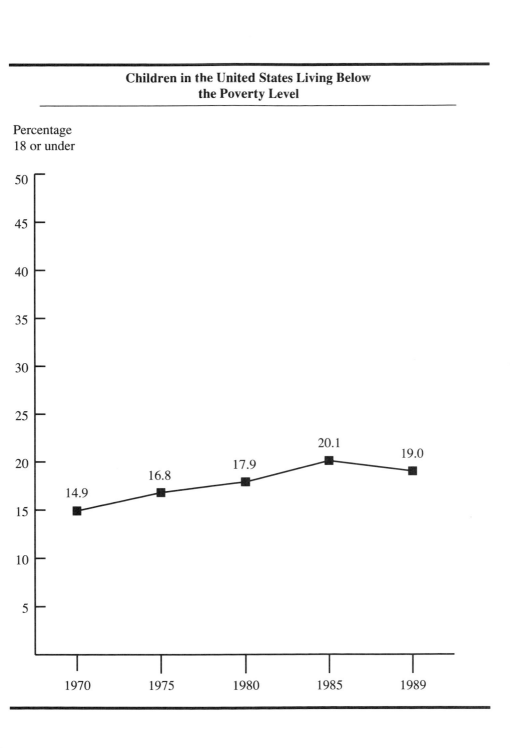

**Children in the United States Living Below
the Poverty Level**

Percentage
18 or under

50 —

45 —

40 —

35 —

30 —

25 —

20 — 14.9   16.8   17.9   20.1   19.0

15 —

10 —

5 —

1970   1975   1980   1985   1989

parent can decide instead to send a child to a private school or a religious school; parents can even educate their child at home or in an alternative program.

Finally, the duty of parents to *control* their children allows parents to make the rules by which their children will live. In fulfilling their duty to control their children, parents may decide who their child's friends will be, when a child or teenager must be home at night, and where that child or teenager may go. Furthermore, parents must stop their children from doing something wrong, such as trespassing or stealing, if they are aware of what their children are doing. This duty to control comes with a right to discipline and punish children, if necessary, in order to force them to obey.

Parents' Rights Over Children

Parents have the right to the *custody* of their children. They have the right to live with and raise their own children. Parents can, however, give someone else this right, even if their children object. Their parental right to custody can also be taken away by a court if the court finds that the parents are unfit to have custody of their children. By virtue of this right to custody, parents have many other rights over their children. For example, parents have the right to choose a child's name and religion.

Children's Duties to Parents

Children have three duties to their parents. Children must obey their parents, render services to their parents, and live with their parents to the age of majority. The *duty to obey* requires children to follow all reasonable orders and rules of their parents. Unreasonable rules are those that would endanger a child's health, safety, or morals. Children must therefore follow rules about what clothes they may wear, when they must be in at night, and what work they must do around the house — even if these rules seem unreasonable to them, so long as the rules do not threaten their health, safety, or morals.

Next, children must *render reasonable services* to their parents. Parents have the right to insist that their children do chores in the home, in the yard, or on the family ranch or farm. Parents can require their children to rake leaves and do other yard work all day on the weekends, but they cannot require their children to rake leaves all night or work at any dangerous task. Such requests would endanger the health of their children. Also, a parent has the right to make a child take a part-time job to help support the family, and can decide what job a child will take, so long as the job does not violate child labor laws.

The *duty to live with parents* until majority requires children in most states to live in their parents' home until the age of eighteen. Children must actually stay in their parents' home or in a home that their parents have selected for them. Thus, when a child is away from home, he or she must be away with parental permission.

Children's Rights in Relation to Parents

Just as parents have the right to the custody of their children, children have the right to be in the custody of their parents and to be raised by their parents. However, children have this right only if their parents agree. Thus, parents can decide to place their children in someone else's custody, regardless of their children's wishes to remain with them. Or a court may order the parents' custody to be terminated.

Children are also protected by law from neglect and abuse by their parents and by persons acting in the role of a parent, such as stepparents, baby-sitters, and the other adults living with the family. Laws making child abuse a crime vary from state to state. Some laws define child abuse as physical abuse or neglect. Some laws include psychological abuse in their

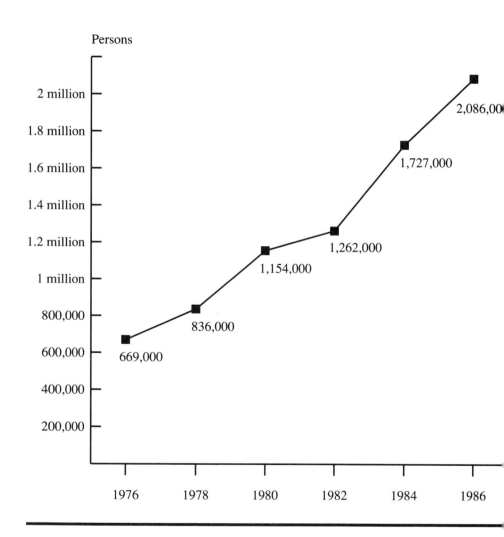

Instances of Child Abuse Reported to U.S. Authorities, 1976-1986

Persons

2 million

1.8 million

1.6 million

1.4 million

1.2 million

1 million

800,000

600,000

400,000

200,000

669,000

836,000

1,154,000

1,262,000

1,727,000

2,086,00

1976   1978   1980   1982   1984   1986

definition of child abuse. Most child abuse laws make it a crime to abuse a child sexually.

Even though laws against child abuse vary, most have a number of common elements. Most include *neglect* in their definition of abuse. Neglect is considered to be something parents do *not* do that the law requires them to do, which results in the endangerment of the child's health, safety, or morals. Neglect is generally defined to be the failure of parents to provide their children with the necessaries of life: food, shelter, clothing, and medical care. Neglect also includes leaving a baby or small child unsupervised, abandoning a child, failing to educate a child, and failing to seek medical care for a sick child. Finally, some states consider a parent's use of drugs or alcohol to constitute neglect.

Abuse is also defined to mean serious physical injury done purposefully. This includes any type of sexual abuse of the child by the parent. Parents who allow another adult to use their child sexually are also guilty of child abuse. Psychological mistreatment of a child is also abuse. Many children suffer imprisonment at the hands of their parents: Some have been locked in a closet or chained to a chair. This type of abuse is both physical and mental.

Because parents have the right to punish their children physically, it is sometimes difficult to determine what constitutes allowable punishment and what is abuse. Parents may hit, spank, or otherwise physically strike their children for the purpose of punishment, but for no other reason. The punishment must be for the welfare and guidance of the child and must always be reasonable and never excessive. Punishments cannot result in great physical injury or mental distress, and they cannot be "cruel and unusual" acts.

In determining whether physical punishment is reasonable and not excessive, parents must consider such factors as the

At home, children learn from adults. (Sally Ann Rogers)

age and health of their child. Spanking a baby who is only two weeks old can be considered excessive and unreasonable; the same spanking given to an eight-year-old may be acceptable. Similarly, spanking a healthy child may be allowed, but spanking an ill child may not be allowed.

Emancipation

Parents and children have these duties and rights to each other during the child's minority, the time before a child reaches the age of majority. Once a child reaches the age of majority, he or she is freed from all parental control and support, and his or her parents have no more rights over, or duties to, the child.

It is possible for parents and children to terminate both their duties to each other and their rights over each other before a child reaches the age of majority. When this occurs, the child becomes *emancipated*. Emancipation requires the consent of both the parents and the child. Parents must agree to give up their rights over their child, and the child must agree to give up his or her parents' support, custody, and protection. Also, the minor involved must be able to care for himself or herself.

Emancipation can be granted by a court. Sometimes parents apply to have their child emancipated so that they can be free of their duties. Usually, however, it is the child who applies to the court for emancipation. In some cases, a child can be emancipated without court permission, but with the express consent of his or her parents. Minors can also be emancipated by the "implied consent" of their parents; a parent who abandons a minor, leaving the minor to care for himself or herself, has given "implied consent." Emancipation automatically occurs when a minor enters military service or gets married.

Chapter Four

Rights at School

Many laws apply to children and schools. Some laws give children privileges and rights, and others give children duties. However, just like parents, the school and its authorities have duties to and rights over students. Because the school is another parental authority, it is said to be acting *in loco parentis* — in place of the parent — when it exercises authority over students.

The Right to Free Public Education

Minors in the United States and Canada have the right to attend public school free of charge. Children have not always enjoyed this privilege. In the nineteenth century, many public schools were started by towns, groups, or individuals. These schools usually charged parents a fee for educating their children. For that reason, schools were usually attended only by wealthy children. Besides, most children had to work to help support their families. At the end of the nineteenth century, however — at about the time reformers and social workers wanted to end child labor — schools began to change. The state of Michigan passed laws making public education free in 1870. Then, in 1872, more high schools were built after the Supreme Court of the United States ruled that government money should be spent for such schools. Soon, many states were passing laws that made education free.

Many children were still not attending school, however, so some states began to require children to attend school. In 1870, only 57 percent of children aged five to seventeen were attending school for some part of the year. In 1918, when Mississippi passed a compulsory attendance law, all states offered free public education and made attendance compulsory.

Therefore, children now have the right to a free public education, but they also have the duty to attend. The right to an education extends even to children who are illegally living in the United States. School attendance is compulsory for all children, from the age of six or seven to the age of sixteen or eighteen. Some states allow minors to leave school earlier once they attain a certain level of education and pass an equivalency test. In Canada, attendance is mandatory for children from the age of six to the age of fifteen or sixteen, depending on the province.

There are some exceptions to compulsory attendance in the United States. First, students need not attend a public school. Parents can send their children to a private school or teach them at home, so long as the program is somewhat similar to that at a public school. Second, students need not attend school if they have a mental or physical problem that makes it impossible for them to attend, if they live far from school and have no transportation, or if they receive vocational training at their job and attend some continuation classes.

Students who fail to attend school when they are required to be in school are *truants*. Truant officers are special police officers who look for children who are not in school during school hours. They return children to school and, if the student is a habitual truant, may arrest that student. A truant officer may also visit parents and try to determine why a child is not in school. Because parents have a duty to ensure that their children are educated, they can be fined if their children are truants.

Rules in School

Because school authorities are *in loco parentis*, standing in the place of parents while students are at school or school-

Since the 1960's "dress codes" at schools have relaxed; students have more rights to express themselves. (John Coletti/Uniphoto)

related functions, they have similar powers over and duties to students. Teachers and principals can punish students to make them obey and are responsible for protecting students' morals, health, and safety. They can make rules governing student behavior.

While the authority of teachers and principals to make rules is great, there are some limitations. First, school rules must be reasonable, which means that they must be connected to educational purposes. Any rules that are intended to prevent harm to students or to the school are reasonable. Rules against behavior that interrupts or distracts students are considered reasonable. Rules can be made against behavior that damages school property, such as painting graffiti on lockers. Also, school authorities can make rules about what students do when they are not on school property, if students are doing something that relates to the school. For example, the school can tell students how to behave at sporting events that do not take place at the school, because those events reflect on the school. The school authorities can also dictate students' behavior when they are coming to school or going home from school. School rules do not need to be written.

In the 1960's, students fought to change some rules that they believed were unfair. For example, many schools once had rules that related to how students could dress and how they could wear their hair. School authorities thought that these regulations were necessary to maintain discipline and prevent disruption. Most schools no longer have such "dress codes," because students challenged these rules, arguing that the rules were vague and unrelated to education and discipline.

Punishment at School

Students may be disciplined and punished in school. There must be good cause for the punishment, and the punishment must be reasonable and related to what the student did wrong.

Thus, a student who brings alcohol to a swim meet can be removed from the team and barred from attending further meets. Teachers and principals can take any special privileges away from students as punishment. However, with all punishments, students have the right to defend themselves and to tell their side of the story.

School authorities are also allowed to punish students physically. This type of punishment, called *corporal punishment*, is very controversial. In 1977, the Supreme Court of the United States decided that the type of physical punishment used in schools does not violate the Eighth Amendment of the Constitution, which forbids "cruel and unusual punishments." However, some states do not allow corporal punishment at all, while other states allow it only under certain conditions, such as only in front of the principal or only as a punishment for certain misbehavior.

When using corporal punishment, teachers and other authorities are limited by constraints. The punishment must be reasonable and cannot be excessive. It can be used only when the authorities know that the student has done something wrong; a mere suspicion of wrongdoing is not sufficient. The punishment cannot be given with malice or as a general threat to get a student to behave. Finally, the school authority who administers the punishment must consider the student's age, sex, and general health.

Other allowable punishments are suspension and expulsion. A school may suspend a student and keep him or her out of school for a short period of time or may expel a student and prohibit that student from attending that school for a year or more. These punishments involve a student's Fourteenth Amendment rights. The Fourteenth Amendment states in part that no state or state authority shall "deprive any person of life, liberty, or property, without due process of law." Before a citizen is denied a liberty such as personal freedom and is sent

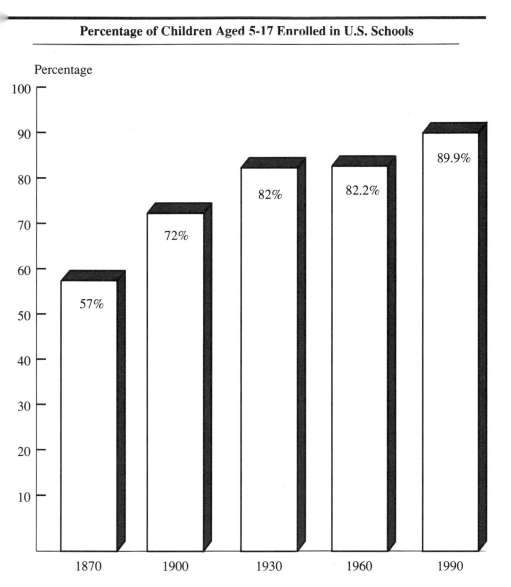

Percentage of Children Aged 5-17 Enrolled in U.S. Schools

Percentage

- 57%
- 72%
- 82%
- 82.2%
- 89.9%

1870   1900   1930   1960   1990

to prison, he or she is guaranteed due process rights such as a trial and an attorney. Likewise, before a student can be suspended or expelled from school, the school authorities must first ensure that the student is given due process rights that allow him a chance to defend himself.

Students did not always have due process rights and could be denied the right to attend public school, without "due process of the law." In 1974, in a case called *Goss v. Lopez*, the Supreme Court applied the due process clause of the Fourteenth Amendment to students who were being suspended. In 1971, a student named Dwight Lopez had been suspended from school in Columbus, Ohio, after a lunchroom disturbance by students that caused damage to school property. Dwight claimed that he was only a bystander. At that same time there were student riots and many other suspensions at two other schools in Columbus. Nine of those students who were suspended, including Dwight, took their cases to court because they had been suspended without a hearing and some had never been told why they were being suspended. The students complained that the Ohio law that allowed a principal to suspend a student was unconstitutional, because it did not give students any due process rights, such as a chance to defend themselves. The Supreme Court agreed that the school, a government agency, could not interfere with a student's right to education without giving him or her the protection of due process. As one of the Supreme Court justices put it, "Young people do not shed their rights at the schoolhouse door."

Because of *Goss v. Lopez*, the suspension or expulsion of a student must follow certain rules. In most states, students who face suspension or expulsion must be given notice and a hearing. A student's parents must also be notified of the charges and the hearing. The student must be told of the evidence the school authorities have, must be given a chance to present his or her side of the story, and may have the right to call witnesses and to have an attorney at the hearing.

Student Records

Schools keep extensive records on students. These records usually include the student's grades, test scores, intelligence test results, health reports, attendance history, behavioral problems, and any comments made by teachers or other school authorities. Until 1974, students did not have any control over their school records. They did not have the right to keep their records private, and neither students nor parents were allowed to view the records. Many students and parents believed that the records could contain unfair or inaccurate information that could be harmful to the student, and it was very difficult for a student or parent to have such information removed. Also, student records were open to police and other law enforcement agencies, such as the Federal Bureau of Investigation.

In 1974, the Family Educational Rights and Privacy Act, commonly called the Buckley Education Amendment, gave students rights over who has access to their records and what goes into the records. While a student is under the age of eighteen, the law limits access to records to the parents or guardians of the student, those to whom the parents give written permission, and school authorities. Police are entitled to see student records without parental permission if they have a lawful court order. Once a student is over the age of eighteen, only that student, those to whom the student gives written permission, and school authorities have access to the records. Finally, either a student or the parents may make a written request to have any information removed from the record that they believe is false or harmful. If the school authorities refuse to remove that information, a statement or letter must be placed in the file explaining that the student or parents disagree with the information and have requested that it be removed.

Free Expression

In the Constitution, the First Amendment guarantees citizens freedom of expression. However, students in public

Children have the right to an education that will prepare them to earn a living. (PhotoBank)

schools were not always considered citizens who enjoyed this right, just as they were not always considered to be among those "citizens" who enjoyed due process protection. Students were given the right of free expression and speech in school in 1969, by a United States Supreme Court case called *Tinker v. Des Moines Independent Community School District.*

In December, 1965, three Iowa teenagers, Mary Beth and John Tinker and their friend Chris Eckhardt, decided to protest the Vietnam War by wearing black armbands during the Christmas season. When public school officials became aware of their plan, they quickly adopted a policy against wearing black armbands: Any student could be suspended for refusing to remove an armband worn to school. When the three students wore their armbands to school anyway, they were suspended. The parents of the children believed that wearing an armband in protest was protected by the First Amendment as free speech that was "symbolic." Symbolic speech is a way to communicate an idea through an action or visual symbol instead of through words or talking, and it is protected by the law just like other forms of speech. The parents said that the suspensions of the three teenagers violated their First Amendment rights to symbolic speech, and they contacted attorneys.

In 1968, the Supreme Court ruled that students have rights of free expression while in school and that those rights were violated when the Tinker and Eckhardt teens were suspended. In their decision, the Court said, "Students in school as well as out of school are persons under our Constitution." The Court held that students could wear armbands or political buttons to school and that students were entitled to express political opinions that differed from those of the school officials.

While students now have freedom of expression in school, some of their expression is still limited. Students do not have the freedom to publish whatever they want in school newspapers. Newspapers and other publications that are sponsored by the school, as part of a class on journalism or as part of a school-sponsored club, can be edited by school officials. Students' rights of free expression are not violated by this type of censorship because the school has an interest in the publications that it sponsors. However, students who publish unofficial newspapers or other materials, outside school and without school sponsorship or help, have more freedom. Students are generally allowed to distribute such newspapers at school so long as the publication does not create a disturbance.

Privacy

Students do not generally have a right to privacy at school. Because the school has an interest in controlling the students and in keeping the students and the school property safe, school authorities may generally search students' lockers or their desks. Courts have decided that because the school (not the student) owns the locker or desk, the student has no right to expect that items in a locker or desk will remain private. Students can be punished or even arrested if something illegal is found in these places. Students do have a right to privacy of their pockets, purses, and "persons" (or bodies). However, the law on this issue is unclear, and different courts have made conflicting decisions.

Chapter Five

Rights at Work

There are limitations on when, where, and how much minors can work. Children have the right not to work until the age of fourteen. Then, when they can work, the type and amount of work they may do is regulated until they reach the age of majority. These limitations generally do not apply to jobs that children frequently do around the home or in the neighborhood, such as housework, yard work, baby-sitting, and washing cars. Limitations on children's ability to work came about as the result of the oppressive child labor practices of the nineteenth century.

Oppressive Labor Practices

Children began to be exploited as workers in factories in the early 1800's, when textile mills opened in New England. In the later part of the nineteenth century, when immigration to the United States and Canada increased dramatically and the production of goods became industrialized, the exploitation of children became extreme. Children have always worked, usually to help support their families. However, although children still worked to help support their families, the type of work changed during the nineteenth century.

The invention of the cotton gin and other farm machinery made small farms unprofitable, so families sent their children to work for others. Children who once worked on small family farms with their parents now worked in cotton fields on huge farms. Children who used to work alongside their parents in family stores or in the home were sent to work in factories. Other children worked in mines.

The number of children who were employed increased. In 1870 in the United States, one out of every eight children worked at a job outside the home. By 1900, one out of every six children was employed. Children in 1910 made up 18 percent of the work force. This count included only those children between the ages of ten and fifteen; many children under the age of ten also worked. Children as young as four labored in textile mills or picked cotton, twelve or thirteen hours a day, seven days a week, every day of the year. Some children even worked at night.

The conditions under which children worked were terrible. For example, nine- and ten-year-old boys who worked in mines frequently had the job of breaker boy. These boys straddled the underground chutes, and as the coal rushed down, they picked out pieces of slate. Breaker boys frequently lost fingers or had their hands crushed; they developed asthma and tuberculosis and eventually became hunchbacked. They had no time to rest, and for lunch they were given a cold potato to eat while they worked. Children who worked in mills frequently had their hair, fingers, and hands pulled off by the machines. The pay that these children received was meager. They did not attend school and could not be out-of-doors during the day. Such children spent most of their young lives in these filthy, dangerous conditions.

Because they could get children to work such long hours at such low rates, the owners of factories, farms, and mines ignored the laws that limited the number of hours that children were allowed to work. They fought any attempt by the government or social workers to enforce those laws. Many in society feared that production of goods was not possible without child labor, so they encouraged the belief that working was good for children.

The Reform of Child Labor

It was not until the end of the nineteenth century that these attitudes began to change. That period is now called the "reform era," when many social workers, journalists, and activists called reformers worked to improve social conditions for exploited groups. Reformers believed that children who worked were victims and that the system deprived these children of their natural rights to education and play. Groups supporting the end of child labor included the American Federation of Labor, the American Medical Association, and the Council of Churches.

Reformers began to fight to change the system and restrict child labor. First, the reformers persuaded Congress that child labor laws had to be changed, and in 1916 Congress passed the Keating-Owens Act. That act prohibited goods that were manufactured by children under the age of fourteen from being shipped interstate (or from state to state) or to a foreign country. To have a successful business, an owner had to be able to ship goods to areas outside the state where they were made, so such a law discouraged child labor. The Keating-Owens Act also prohibited *any* labor by children under the age of fourteen, and it limited the hours that children aged fourteen to sixteen could work to eight hours per day.

Factory owners and other big-business people fought back. In 1918, the Keating-Owens Act was declared unconstitutional by the Supreme Court. Many justices on the Supreme Court were sympathetic to business owners, and one stated that the law violated children's "freedom" to work. In making their decision, the justices did not consider the conditions under which children worked. Later, in 1919, Congress tried again to outlaw child labor by putting a 10 percent tax on the owners' profits from goods manufactured by children. This law was also declared unconstitutional by the Supreme Court.

Then, in 1924, the reformers tried to end child labor by adding an amendment to the Constitution. The proposed

Young children, like this paperboy, may work at some types of jobs. (Ed Elberfeld/Uniphoto)

amendment gave Congress the power to limit, regulate, and prohibit work by persons under the age of eighteen. However, the amendment was not ratified by enough of the states to be added to the Constitution. Those opposed to the amendment called it a communist and socialist plot and said that it invaded the home and took away parents' and states' rights.

Finally, reformers decided to fight child labor by insisting that states enforce their school attendance laws. By 1918, all states had compulsory attendance laws, and once these laws began to be enforced, child labor began to decline. Still, it was not until 1938, when Congress passed the Fair Labor Standards Act, that child labor for children under fourteen was expressly abolished and, for children over fourteen, was regulated. The Supreme Court later upheld this law. One of its provisions was similar to the Keating-Owens Act of 1916, prohibiting the interstate shipment of goods made by children under the age of fourteen and the full-time employment of children under the age of sixteen. The Fair Labor Standards Act, which has been amended many times since 1938, also limits the type of jobs minors can hold.

Limitations on Children's Work

In the United States, children are protected from "oppressive labor practices" by the Fair Labor Standards Act and by different state laws. In some instances, state laws are even stricter about when, where, and how much children can work, while in other states, the laws are the same as the federal law. In Canada, each province limits the number of hours children can work and enforces a minimum age at which children can begin to work.

First, children in the United States generally cannot work until the age of fourteen. Fourteen- and fifteen-year-olds are limited to working three-hour days and eighteen-hour weeks when school is in session. When school is not in session, those teens may usually work up to eight hours per day and forty hours per week. They may not work any overtime hours and cannot work at night. Sixteen-year-olds may work up to four hours per day and twenty hours per week when school is in session. When school is not in session, they are allowed to work up to eight hours per day and forty-eight hours per week. The extra eight hours over a usual forty-hour week must be paid at the adult overtime rate and must be worked on an additional day. These rules are the usual rules and may vary from state to state. In most states, minors are prohibited from working from 7:00 P.M. to 7:00 A.M. Many states permit children below the age of fourteen to work at certain, specified jobs, such as golf caddying and delivering newspapers.

Next, both federal and state laws forbid children of any age from working in dangerous jobs. Only those over the age of eighteen can work at these jobs. Under the Fair Labor Standards Act, children may not work at the following jobs:

- coal mining or any job in a mine
- logging and sawmill jobs
- driving a motor vehicle or working as a driver's outside helper
- excavating
- roofing
- wrecking and demolition
- manufacturing and storing explosives
- slaughtering and meat packing
- dangerous exhibitions, such as certain circus acts
- manufacturing bricks and tile
- operating bakery machines, paper product machines, power-driven metal-forming machines, power-driven saws and shears, and power-driven hoisting machines

Some states also prevent children from working at other dangerous jobs. For example, Illinois considers working in

In 1905, children could still be exploited for their labor. (Collection of Deborah Cooney)

bowling alleys, billiard rooms, and gas stations too dangerous for anyone under the age of sixteen. In New York, those under eighteen years of age cannot work in dry-cleaning businesses or in any job that uses a poisonous or radioactive substance.

Some jobs are not covered by child labor laws. Children work at these jobs without any regulation or limitation. Jobs such as house cleaning, yard work, and baby-sitting are not covered. Most agricultural work is not covered, and today many minors work in the fields under the same conditions that child labor laws sought to prevent.

Finally, most child labor laws do not apply to minors of any age who work as professional actors, actresses, models, or athletes. Minors are generally permitted to work at these jobs at any age, under the supervision of a parent or guardian. Children may even take some acting jobs at night. Some states have specific labor provisions for these jobs, relating to how many hours children may work at them, their education, their contracts, and their salaries.

Earnings

Most jobs are covered by what is called the "minimum hourly wage": the least amount of money that can be paid an employee for each hour worked. The minimum wage changes occasionally and is set by both federal and state law. Most of the jobs that minors take — jobs in fast-food restaurants and movie theaters, for example — are covered by the minimum wage. However, minimum wage laws do not apply to housework, baby-sitting, yard work, and some farm jobs. Minimum wage also does not apply to jobs done on a infrequent or irregular basis.

Regardless of how much money employed minors earn, in most states parents are entitled to collect those earnings. Because parents have a duty to support their children, they also have a right to use the earnings of their children to help support those children. Therefore, parents of children who do not live at home can collect a child's earnings so long as they are fully supporting that child. In general, parents do not have the right to collect their child's earnings if they are not fully supporting their child. Also, in some states, parents lose the right to these earnings if they have ever let their child keep them in the past; in other states, parents can collect the earnings only if they notify their child's employer that they intend to do so. However, parents and children can make any agreement about the child's earnings that they want. Some states permit child actors, actresses, models, and athletes to keep their own earnings. Often these earnings must be kept by law in a special fund for the child until the age of majority.

Chapter Six

Rights in Court

A child can become involved in the court system in many different ways. The child may commit a crime, may commit what is called a "status offense" (an act that is an offense only if a minor commits it), or may be abused and in need of the court's protection. Regardless of how a child comes to the court system, he or she will be treated differently from an adult. A completely different criminal system, called the *juvenile justice system*, deals with children who need court supervision or commit crimes.

The Juvenile Court Philosophy

Until the twentieth century, children who came to the attention of the police were treated as adults. Regardless of what they did — whether they committed a theft or ran away from home — children were tried as adults and were locked up in jail with adults. Children as young as eight were executed for such crimes as arson and murder. Many social reformers found this practice to be inhumane and fought for the establishment of a separate justice system for minors, or *juveniles*.

In 1899, Illinois established the first court system for juveniles. The idea behind this separate system of procedures for juveniles was *parens patriae* (literally, "father of the country," referring to the power of the government over those citizens who have a disability, such as youth). Thus, the court system would act as a parent in dealing with a child who had committed a crime or had been neglected or abused. The child was not to be treated as a criminal, but as a child, or *ward*, of the court. One reformer stated that a child coming into the juvenile justice system "shall be treated, not as a criminal, but as misdirected and misguided, and needing aid, encouragement, help and assistance." This change in the Illinois system was hailed by society as a great advance and was copied by other states. By 1909, thirty-five states had separate juvenile court systems, and by the 1920's, almost every state had legal provisions for treating juveniles in the court system differently from adults.

The goal of the juvenile court system is to rehabilitate and help, rather than punish. The system assumes that conditions beyond the child's control may have pushed the child into crime, and it seeks to give the child needed services and counseling so that the child's life can be made better. The juvenile court system assumes that the court and the judge are acting as a parent and are not against the child. Social workers, psychologists, and counselors all work in the juvenile court system.

Who Goes to Juvenile Court?

First, to be treated by the separate juvenile court system, one must be a juvenile. The juvenile court system is generally available to children under the age of eighteen, although in some states only children under the age of sixteen or seventeen may be tried in juvenile court. Also, many states allow children who commit serious crimes — such as murder or armed robbery — to be tried as adults, in the adult criminal system. Some states allow children as young as ten, and others allow children aged thirteen and older, to be transferred to adult court after a hearing for such a serious crime.

Juveniles can come under the jurisdiction (or care of) the juvenile justice system in two primary ways: Some juveniles are under the court's jurisdiction because they have committed a "status offense" and are considered to be in need of supervision by the court. Others are in the court system because they have committed a crime. These juveniles are sometimes referred to as delinquents.

Persons in Need of Supervision

Children who are in need of supervision by the court are called "persons in need of supervision," or PINS. A PINS is a juvenile who has committed a status offense. PINS are also referred to as status offenders.

A *status offense* is an action that is not against the law for an adult but is prohibited for a minor. Status offenses include running away from home, being truant from school, having sexual relations, and drinking alcohol. Minors who commit these offenses are considered "incorrigible" and beyond the control of their parents or guardians. A minor must generally commit several status offenses, or be habitually in trouble at school or home, to be considered a status offender or PINS. Some children and lawyers have challenged status offenses as unconstitutional because they subject children to restrictions on personal behavior (adults do not have these restrictions). However, courts have upheld status offenses as constitutional.

PINS and status offense laws were drafted to help parents control their children. Parents or police or school officials can charge a child with a status offense and seek to have that child declared a person in need of supervision by filing a petition with the juvenile court. When a PINS petition is filed, a hearing must be held: The parent, the minor, the person making the petition, and the judge meet in the judge's room or chamber. In most states, the minor has the right to have a lawyer present to represent him or her. Both the minor and the person who is seeking to have the court take the minor as a PINS have a chance to speak and explain their positions. The

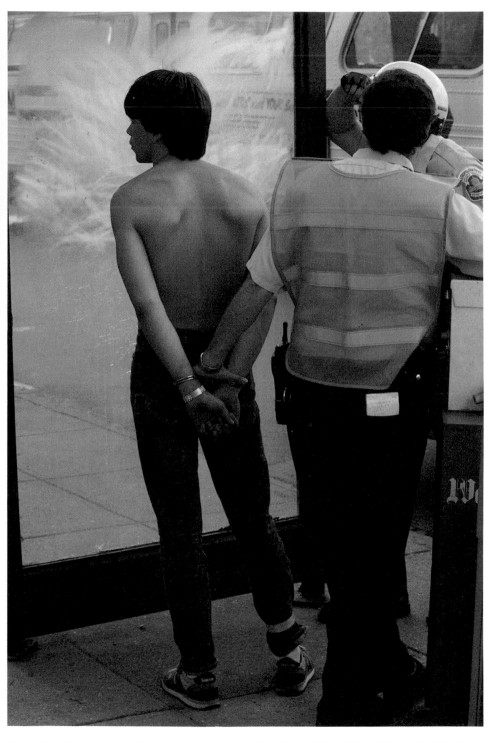

Juveniles who commit crimes can be arrested, just like adults. (Mark Reinstein/Uniphoto)

judge then decides if the minor is in need of supervision.If a minor is declared a PINS, he or she is usually placed on probation. While on probation, the minor must report to a probation officer and obey the rules the judge makes. The judge may make rules about attending school, curfew, what friends the minor may see, and where he or she can go besides home and school. If a PINS violates the probation rules, he or she may be put in a training school, foster home, state camp, or group home, or may be treated by the state as a delinquent.

Juveniles Who Commit Crimes

Juveniles who are arrested for committing crimes are called *delinquents*. After arrest, juveniles are tried and detained by the juvenile court system. Although the court process for juveniles is very different from that for adults, some court decisions have begun to make the juvenile system more like the adult system by giving juveniles the protection of rules. A case decided by the Supreme Court in 1967, *In re Gault*, gave juveniles a number of rights after arrest that they did not previously have.

The Case of Gerald Gault

In Arizona, in June of 1964, fifteen-year-old Gerald Gault was arrested after making an obscene phone call to the Gaults' neighbor. The neighbor notified the police and identified Gerald as the caller. Much later, Gerald stated that even though he had dialed the phone number, a friend of his was the one who had spoken to the neighbor. Gerald's parents were not notified that their son had been arrested and that Gerald was in detention. After missing Gerald, Gerald's mother finally contacted the sheriff and was told that he had been arrested and that a hearing would be held the next afternoon. Gerald apparently confessed to making the call while he was alone with a police officer, but he was never given a chance to talk to his parents and was never told that he had a right to speak to a lawyer and the right to remain silent. Neither Gerald nor his parents were shown the petition filed at the hearing, and the neighbor reporting the crime was not at the hearing to give evidence. Neither Gerald nor his parents knew that they could have had a lawyer represent them at the hearing. The judge declared that Gerald was a delinquent and sentenced him to a state school for "the period of his minority," which was until he was twenty-one. Gerald was given a six-year sentence for making an obscene phone call.

Gerald and his parents appealed his sentence. They believed that Gerald had been treated unfairly because he was a juvenile and that his constitutional rights to due process of law — such as having a lawyer present and confronting his accuser — had been violated. In May of 1967, the Supreme Court decided that the juvenile court's decision that Gerald was a delinquent was improper. Gerald was released after spending almost three years at the state school.

Due Process for Juveniles

The Supreme Court decided that Gerald's Fourteenth Amendment right to due process had been violated. The Court ruled that children must be given proper notice of charges against them, that children have a right to counsel, that children have the right against self-incrimination (the right not to speak), and that they must be informed of these rights. The Court also ruled that at a juvenile court hearing, the judge must swear in witnesses against the juvenile and must allow cross-examination of any witnesses. When a juvenile is arrested, he or she must be told of these rights. After arrest, the police are required to contact the arrested child's parents and notify them of what has happened.

Court Hearings

After arrest, a juvenile may be released to his or her parents and the matter may be dropped. Or, the juvenile may be placed in the custody of his or her parents until the time of the hearing on the matter. The juvenile may also be held in custody until the hearing.

In the juvenile court system, there are generally three hearings. The first hearing is the *initial hearing*. The juvenile and the parents must be given proper notice of the date of the initial hearing and of the charges against the juvenile. At the initial hearing, the state must prove to the court that a crime has been committed and that there is reasonable cause to believe that the juvenile who was arrested committed it. If the juvenile is in custody, this hearing must take place within two to four days. If the court finds that there is reasonable evidence, the juvenile may be sent home with his or her parents until the second hearing, called the *adjudicatory hearing*. If the court decides to keep the juvenile in custody, a *detention hearing* must also be held. The detention hearing determines where the juvenile will be placed in custody. If the court decides that there is not reasonable evidence that the juvenile committed the offense with which he or she has been charged, the court can release the juvenile. Or the court can, for other reasons, decide to drop the matter entirely if appropriate.

At the adjudicatory hearing, the court decides whether or not the juvenile is guilty of the crime charged. All hearings in the juvenile court system are closed to everyone except the juvenile, the parents, the judge, the lawyer for the state, the juvenile's lawyer, any witnesses, and the probation officer or social worker. The name of the juvenile and the details of the accusation are kept private. In all but a few states, the juvenile is not given the right to a trial by jury; instead, the judge decides his or her guilt, because the judge is assumed to be on the child's side. If the judge determines that the juvenile is not guilty, the child is released. If the juvenile is found guilty, there must be a *dispositional hearing*.

At the dispositional hearing, the court decides what will happen to the juvenile. The probation department prepares a report on the child that considers the child's family background, psychological background, school background, and social background. Factors such as whether the child was abused or neglected, suffers from psychiatric problems, has learning disabilities, or was previously arrested are considered. The judge then has a number of options in deciding how to sentence the juvenile.

Sentencing and Detention

The juvenile may be put on *probation*. If on probation, the juvenile may live at home or may be placed in a foster home if the home environment will not be supportive of the juvenile or may encourage further criminal activity. The juvenile may also be placed in a group home or a state or county camp. Juveniles in these detention settings may be assigned to a probation officer who is responsible for them. If the juvenile violated the law after living in a foster or group home or camp, he or she may be placed in a juvenile hall, and receive much more supervision. If the juvenile has committed an even more serious crime, he or she may be sent to a state correctional institution. These facilities usually do not provide a home environment, counseling, or other services. Here, juveniles are constantly supervised and kept in *maximum confinement*, just as they would be in a jail or a prison.

Regardless of the type of detention given to juveniles, they have the same rights during their detention as they had when they were not being detained. In a foster home, group home, or state camp, juveniles have the right to adequate food, clothing, medical care, and education. In a juvenile hall or correctional institution, juveniles have these rights and rights to such things as regular visitation with parents and others, sanitary living conditions such as clean bedding, access to a library and reading material, freedom from overcrowding, and adequate recreational exercise periods.

Children who are detained also have the right not to be placed in adult jails. States are prohibited from regularly placing juvenile offenders with adult offenders, but many continue to place children in adult jails under certain circumstances. Some states place children in adult jails but make sure that the child has no contact with adult prisoners or that the child is not in a cell with an adult. Other states allow children to be placed in adult facilities only if no juvenile facilities are available. Adult facilities are not intended for children and do not provide the services that children may need, such as counseling or educational and recreational facilities. Also, children in adult jails are exposed to serious, dangerous criminals, who may injure or sexually assault them, and are forced into extremely punitive conditions that run counter to the philosophies of the juvenile court system.

Court Records

Because the juvenile offender is to be rehabilitated instead of punished, the law keeps a juvenile's court history private. Records of a juvenile's hearings and detention are sealed or destroyed. Once a juvenile reaches the age of majority, many states allow the former juvenile offender to tell employers and others that he or she has no criminal record. After the juvenile reaches the age of majority, these states seal the court records of these proceedings as if they had never happened. In other states, a former offender is considered not to have a criminal record, but to have only a delinquent or "youthful offender" record.

Abused Children

Children, as we have seen, can enter the court system by committing a status offense or a crime. A third way that a child may come under the jurisdiction of the juvenile justice system is if the child is abused or neglected by his or her parents or guardians. Such a child is usually first referred to the county's social welfare agency, and a social worker is assigned to the case. That person must decide whether the child should be removed from the home. If the social worker determines that the child is in imminent danger of being injured again, the child can be removed immediately. However, if the situation is not an emergency situation, there must be a hearing by a juvenile court judge before the child may be taken from his or her parents.

At a hearing to determine whether a child should be temporarily removed from a home where abuse or neglect is suspected, both the parents and the social worker have a right to speak. The parents must be given enough notice of the hearing to be able to prepare a defense. The parents have a right to have a lawyer represent them, and the social welfare agency is represented by a lawyer as well. The social worker and the social welfare agency lawyer are said to represent the "interest of the state" in protecting children. The child usually has the right to be represented separately as well.

Children at such hearings did not always have the right to be represented. It was thought that the social worker and agency lawyer, representing the state, also represented the child's interest. However, the state and the child may not always have the same interest, and the social worker and child may have a difference of opinion about what should happen to the child. The social worker may want to put the child in a foster home, but the child may want to live with a relative instead. The social worker may believe that the child should be removed from his or her parents, but the child may want to stay with them. Therefore, children generally now have the right to be represented by a *guardian ad litem* (literally, a "guardian for the lawsuit"). A guardian ad litem may be an attorney, a social worker, or a trained volunteer. The guardian ad litem is charged with representing the child's interest and with making sure that the court knows how the child feels about the matter being decided.

When a child has been abused, the state may also take criminal action against the person who abused the child. Frequently, the child must testify in court about the abuse. There have been attempts to make it easier for children to go through this process, which can be especially confusing and painful: A child may feel as though he or she is on trial or under attack or is responsible for the breakup of the family. Generally, a child will be very frightened, both of his abuser and of the court process itself. States have therefore attempted to make it easier for children to testify.

Some states allow children to use dolls to show the court or jury where or how they were abused, while some courts allow the testifying child to sit on a supportive adult's lap. Some states have experimented with allowing the child to testify in another room and transmitting the testimony to the courtroom via closed-circuit television. The constitutionality of this method has been questioned, because people accused of a crime have the constitutional right to "confront" the person accusing them — here the child — and this system may violate that right. The problems faced by children who have been abused and have to testify in court also may affect children who witness a crime and testify in court.

Chapter Seven

Rights in the Community

Children have many rights in their community in addition to their rights at home, at school, on the job, or in the juvenile court system. These rights govern children's relationships to those other than parents, teachers, and employers. Community rights include children's rights to transact business and their legal rights and obligations to others.

The Right to Transact Business

Children have rights that relate to their ability to make, avoid, and enforce contracts; to their money; to their possessions; and to their ability to own property.

Contracts

Children have the right to enter into contracts — whether or not these contracts are written — to purchase goods, to perform services, or to have services performed for them. For example, a minor can make a contract to buy a bicycle on credit, to wash a neighbor's car every week, or to have an artist paint his or her portrait. When a minor makes a contract with an adult, the adult is bound to the contract, meaning that he or she must do what was promised in the contract. However, minors can

Children have the right to transact business. (Bob Daemmrich/Uniphoto)

back out of most contractual agreements that they make. Thus, contracts made by minors are *voidable*; the minor can void, or "disaffirm," the contract.

Therefore, if a child enters into an agreement for the sale of a stereo but later decides that she does not have enough money to pay for it, the child can disaffirm the contract. The child must return the stereo and is entitled to get back the money already paid, with a deduction for the wear and tear on the stereo. The law allows children to get out of contracts that they have made, but it does not allow them to disaffirm the contract and still enjoy the benefits of the contract, such as the stereo. The child must return the stereo; she may not keep it.

Some contracts that minors enter into are not voidable, however. A marriage contract made by a minor who marries with parental permission is binding. So is a contract made by a minor entering the armed forces. Contracts made by minors operating their own businesses are generally enforceable by adults if the contract is fair and reasonable. Most states have special laws that make contracts binding when children are working as actors or actresses, as models, or as professional athletes.

Another exception to the rule that contracts with minors are voidable by the minor concerns contracts made by minors for "necessaries," that is, things necessary for the welfare and health of the child, such as food, clothing, shelter, and medical care. If a parent is not providing these things to a child, a child may make a contract for them. The child cannot disaffirm a contract for necessaries, and such a contract is binding on both the child and his or her parents. This exception to the rule has been made so that children can get the things that they really need to survive.

Because minors can void contracts that they have made, most adults will not do business with them. It is usually too risky for a businessperson to make a contract with a minor when the minor can get out of the contract. The rule on necessaries ensures that businesses will provide these things to minors, because these businesses have the assurance that the minor and his or her parents will be bound by the agreement. Therefore, while the rule on contracts protects children who enter into contracts that they later want to disaffirm, it also makes it difficult for children to do business.

Money

Parents are generally entitled to keep a child's earnings, but children do have rights to their own money. Children may have their own money because parents have allowed them to keep their earnings. When children receive money from gifts or by inheritance, that money is their own, and their parents have no right to it. In some instances, when children inherit a great deal of money, a parent or other adult may be required to supervise the money and how it is used. In some circumstances, children can also keep money that is awarded to them in lawsuits.

When children have their own money, they are entitled to open a bank account in their own name. Their parents' names do not have to be on the account. Parents do not have to give permission for the account to be opened; in fact, parents do not have to be told about the account at all. Children can withdraw or add to the money in their accounts and can generally spend it in any way they like, so long as it is legal.

Children who are receiving an income — whether or not their parents are keeping their earnings — must, however, pay income tax, like everyone else. If a child has a job, taxes are usually withheld from the paycheck. The child may then file a tax return if too much money has been withheld and should receive a refund from the government. The child who is receiving interest income from money that has been invested must also pay taxes on that interest.

Teenagers have the right to own real property, such as cars, and the obligation to drive safely. (Henley Savage/Uniphoto)

Possessions

Children are entitled to own both *personal property*, such as clothing, records, books, bicycles, and cars, and *real property*, such as land, houses, or other buildings. Clothing and furniture provided to children by parents are the property of parents, while toys and books given to children, or records and bicycles purchased by children, are their own possessions. Although children are entitled to own real property, they are generally not allowed to manage or control it. Therefore, a child may not rent, sell, or otherwise manage or dispose of real estate until the age of majority. Real property owned by children is generally managed by a parent or trustee for the benefit of the child. A trustee is an adult hired by a child's parents or guardians to manage the property until the child reaches a certain age.

Wills

While a child can generally spend his or her own money as desired, a child cannot decide what will happen to the money should he or she die. Minors in most states do not have the right to make a will — a document that stipulates what happens to their money and possessions when they die — until they reach a certain age. The age at which a child may make a will may or may not be the age of majority. When a child dies, his or her money and possessions go to a relative, usually a parent if one is living, or, if not, a sibling.

Legal Rights and Obligations

Children can be sued by others, and they have the right to sue those who violate their rights or who injure them. In any civil lawsuit, a child who is being sued or who sues someone else has the right to have a lawyer represent him. A "civil" wrong may be a physical injury to someone else or an injury to someone else's property. An injury to someone's reputation is also a civil wrong. A civil wrong is called a *tort*.

Torts can happen in many different ways. They can be committed by accident or by recklessness. A person can intentionally commit a tort and harm someone else. Often, torts are the result of *negligence*, which is the legal term for carelessness. A tort occurs through negligence when someone does something careless and an injury results, as when a child is riding her bicycle without holding onto the handlebars and crashes into another person. This is a negligent act, even if it was unintentional and even if the child tried to stop the crash before it occurred.

Torts that frequently involve children include traffic accidents, where children are riding bicycles or walking;

trespassing, when children go onto someone else's property without permission; libel and slander, which cause injury to another person's reputation; assault and battery; and nuisances. To commit *libel* is to print something false and damaging about someone else; to commit *slander* is to say (rather than print) such damaging information. *Assault* is a verbal threat or attack made on another person, while *battery* is physically beating or using force on another person. *Nuisances* are things that annoy or disturb others, such as loud noises, smells, bright lights, and animals.

All children over the age of six or seven are responsible for their actions that cause injury to someone else. In some states, children over the age of four are legally responsible for any civil wrongs they commit. They are expected to be careful and not be reckless when doing things that can result in an injury to someone else. However, when determining whether a child has been negligent, a court considers whether the action done by the child is negligent *for a child of that age*. For example, if a seven-year-old is accused of being negligent because he ran into someone while riding a bicycle, the court would consider whether running into that person was a negligent act for a seven-year-old, and whether most seven-year-olds would know that what they were doing was likely to cause an injury to someone else.

There are some exceptions to a child's responsibility for his or her civil wrongs. Children are not responsible for their actions if they are following the suggestion or direction of a parent, or if they are doing something with a parent's permission, or if the negligence of the parent allows the child to do the act, or if a parent knows that the child is doing a wrongful act and fails to stop the child. Also, in some states, parents, not the children themselves, are responsible for the *malicious mischief* of their children. Malicious mischief includes such things as petty vandalism, breaking car windows, and destroying property.

When a child causes someone else to be injured by committing a civil wrong, that child can be sued by the injured person. When a civil lawsuit is brought, the injured person seeks damages for the injury suffered. Here, "damages" means money. If the injured person had medical bills because of physical injuries or repair bills because of damaged property, he or she would ask for money to compensate for these expenses. An injured person can also ask the court to award damages to compensate for emotional upset as a result of the injury. Because it may be difficult to collect money damages from a child, many people try to sue the child's parents instead of the child. However — with the exceptions listed above — parents are not generally responsible for the civil wrongs committed by their children. Also, when a child owes money damages as a result of a lawsuit, only he or she owes it; parents are not required to pay money owed by their children as a result of a lawsuit.

Sometimes children themselves are injured by a civil wrong and may sue the person who injured them. However, children lack what is called the "legal capacity to sue." This does not mean that children cannot initiate a civil lawsuit, but a person over the age of majority must bring the lawsuit for them. A lawsuit brought by an adult for a minor is in the minor's name. The person bringing the suit is often the parent but may be a lawyer or a friend. Children have the same rights as adults to recover damages. In general, any money they receive as damages is their own money, not their parents'. However, when parents have paid medical bills for a child's injury or have paid to have a child's property replaced after it has been damaged, the parents are entitled to take from the child's damages the amount that they have paid out. Or, if an employed child suffers an injury that causes him or her to miss work and receives wages lost in damages, the parents are entitled to collect that amount in damages if they have been collecting their child's earnings all along.

Young people may participate in public demonstrations. (Bob Daemmrich/Uniphoto)

Besides being able to sue acquaintances and strangers who negligently injure them, children may be allowed to sue members of their own families. In some states, children can sue their own parents for negligent conduct. Courts have found that parents have no right to act negligently toward their children. Children most commonly sue their parents for injuries that result when they are involved in a car accident in which their parents were at fault. Parents may encourage this type of lawsuit because then the parents' insurance policy would pay for the child's injury. However, children are not allowed to sue their parents for any negligent act. Most courts do not allow children to sue their parents for making wrong decisions about how to raise the child or merely for being incompetent parents. Children can also sue their minor brothers and sisters for negligence that results in injury.

Children are usually allowed to sue their parents for injuries that are the result of the parent's *intentional* actions — for something that the parent did on purpose. Thus, children can sue their parents for personal injuries that result from physical abuse or intentional neglect. They can also sue their parents for damage to their personal property. A child may have to wait until the age of majority to sue his or her parents or may have to ask a court for limited emancipation for the purpose of suing his parents.

Finally, a child, like an adult, has the right to an undamaged reputation. This means that a child can bring an action against anyone who has committed libel or slander and has harmed the child's reputation. Minors have successfully sued for libel and slander in many different cases, including one case in which someone told a boy's father in a letter that the boy had a venereal disease, a case in which a newspaper wrote that a minor "hangs around in a disreputable part of town," and a case in which someone stated that an unmarried girl was pregnant.

Chapter Eight

Rights
in
Relationships

The law governs minors' rights and freedoms in their most
personal relationships: their relationships with each other.
Laws govern a minor's right to have sexual relations, to marry,
and to receive medical treatment for venereal disease and birth
control. Laws also determine how girls can respond to a
pregnancy. While the law in some ways protects minors'
freedoms and access to information and treatment, it also
makes the act of sexual intercourse illegal for most minors.

Sexual Relations

In general, it is illegal for minors to have sex with each
other or for an adult to have sex with a minor. This is true even
if both partners consent to having sex and neither partner is
forcing the other to have sex. Intercourse for minors is illegal
because of statutory rape laws. *Statutory rape* laws make
sexual intercourse with a minor below the age of consent
illegal. These laws are intended to protect minors (usually just
minor girls) by making it illegal to have sex with a minor.
Such laws assume that minors are incapable of consenting to
sex with a full understanding of what they are consenting to do.
Thus, any act of sex involving a minor is rape, or forced sex.

Teenagers Having Abortions in the United States, 1973-1987

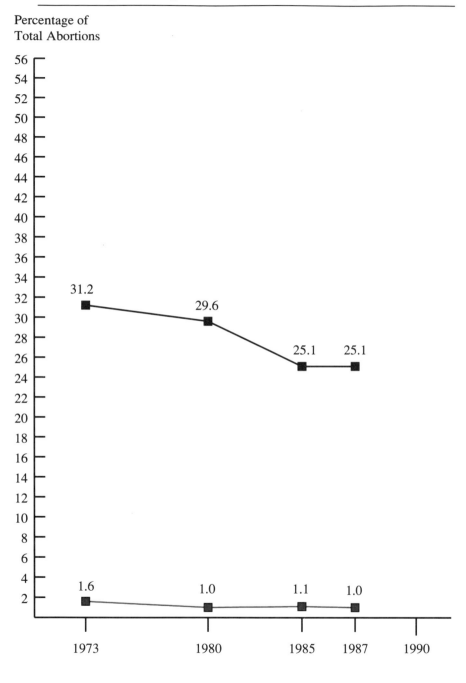

Percentage of
Total Abortions

Girls aged 15-19.

Girls under age 15.

Births to Teenage Mothers in the United States, 1970-1988

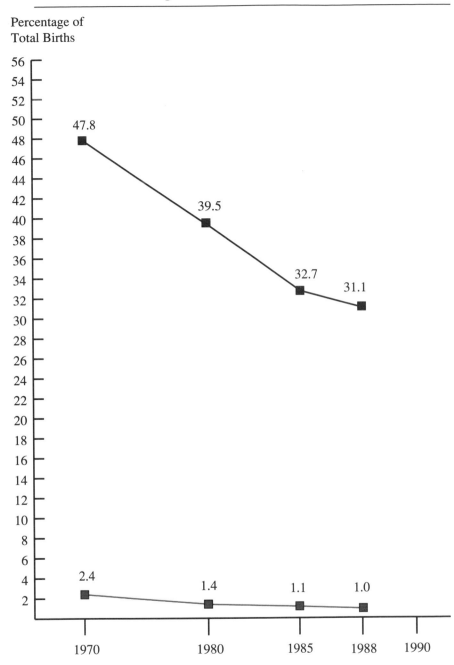

Percentage of
Total Births

56
54
52
50 — 47.8
48
46
44
42 — 39.5
40
38
36 — 32.7
34 — 31.1
32
30
28
26
24
22
20
18
16
14
12
10
8
6
4 — 2.4
2 — 1.4   1.1   1.0

1970   1980   1985   1988   1990

Girls aged 15-19.

Girls under age 15.

The *age of consent* — below which minors are considered to be unable to consent to sex — varies from state to state, but it is usually sixteen. In some states the age of consent is as low as twelve or thirteen years of age, and in some states it is as high as eighteen. While statutory rape laws are generally intended to protect girls, a few states include boys under their statutory rape laws, so that any person who has sex with a boy under the age of consent is also guilty of rape. In 1981, the California law on statutory rape was challenged in the United States Supreme Court as discriminatory. The California law prohibited only men and boys from having sex with minor girls, but it did not prohibit women and girls from having sex with minor boys. The Supreme Court decided that the law was not discriminatory, because girls, the Court said, risk more (such as pregnancy) when they have sex, and the California law was intended to prevent teen pregnancies. By making it illegal for boys and men to have sex with minor girls, statutory rape laws make sexual relations between minor couples illegal.

Most states also have an age of prosecution as part of their statutory rape laws. The age of prosecution is the age above which someone can be charged with committing statutory rape. In most states, a minor can be prosecuted for statutory rape once he or she is over the age of fourteen. In some states, minors of any age can be prosecuted for statutory rape. When the girl involved is younger than a certain age — usually eleven years of age — the boy or man involved can be charged with a more serious crime than statutory rape: *forced rape*. The sentence for forced rape is more severe and usually involves a prison sentence.

In general, statutory rape occurs whenever a minor under the age of consent has had sexual intercourse. The law considers this fact only and does not consider any excuses or defenses of those involved. However, in a few states, statutory rape laws apply only when the minor girl involved was a virgin before she had intercourse illegally. In other states, if it can be proved that the girl involved convinced the boy or man that she was older than the age of consent (through behavior such as drinking in a bar), the laws do not apply. While statutory laws exist in every state, they are rarely used to prosecute minors below the age of consent who have sexual relations. Prosecutions occur most often when parents complain or when the age difference between the minor girl and boy or man is great.

Even when two minors are above the age of consent, the law restricts their sexual activities. In some states, it is illegal for unmarried persons to have sexual relations. Other states forbid unmarried couples to live together. Many states have laws prohibiting homosexual sex.

Marriage

Every state has laws that regulate when minors may marry without their parents' permission. In most states, minors must be eighteen years of age before they can marry without the permission of their parents. In a few states, minors must be nineteen or twenty-one to marry without permission. In a few other states, minors over the age of sixteen may marry without their parents' permission.

When underage minors marry without their parents' consent, the marriage is either void or voidable. In some states, such a marriage is *void*, which means that the marriage does not exist legally at all — it is as if it never took place. In states where a marriage between two minors is *voidable*, the marriage exists unless someone complains to a court about it. Usually, it is the parents or family members of one of the minors who complain that the minors married without permission. Then the court can void that marriage.

When minors who are married are still of school age, they may generally continue to attend public school, although they

School dances are where many young people begin relationships. (Tommy Noonan/
Uniphoto)

are not required to do so in some states. Some schools have attempted to exclude married minors from attending because officials believed that married students may disturb other students and jeopardize the school routine. However, courts have ruled that this law is unreasonable.

When a child or teenager under the age of majority marries without parental permission when allowed to or marries with permission, he or she is automatically emancipated from his or her parents. The parents are freed of their obligation to support their child, and the child is free from parental control. If a minor who was married becomes separated from or abandoned by his or her spouse before reaching the age of majority, that child's parents are required to support the child again, if no other support is available.

Medical Treatment

In general, no doctor or other medical professional may treat a child under the age of majority without the permission of that child's parents, unless the child is emancipated or the situation is an emergency. However, most states recognize special circumstances that allow children to seek medical treatment without the permission of their parents. For example, most states allow children to seek treatment for drug and alcohol addiction without parental permission, and many allow children to seek mental health treatment without permission. Other special circumstances include treatment for venereal disease and treatment for birth control purposes.

Minors in every state can be examined and treated for venereal diseases such as syphilis, gonorrhea, and herpes simplex without parental permission. Most states allow minors of every age to obtain such treatment, while a few states allow only those minors over the age of twelve or fourteen to do so. A doctor who treats a minor child for venereal diseases does not need to notify the minor's parents of the treatment.

While treatment or counseling for venereal disease is kept confidential and is not revealed to a minor's parents, a doctor may be required by the state to file a report with a public health agency. These agencies keep track of the number of cases of venereal disease and where the disease appears. These reports are made regardless of whether the person seeking treatment is a minor or an adult. The public health agency receiving the report keeps the name and circumstances of the patient private.

Similarly, minors have the right to obtain birth control without parental permission. Their rights are different depending on whether they are seeking nonprescription or prescription birth control. No state restricts the sale of nonprescription forms of birth control, such as condoms and spermicides. A decision by the United States Supreme Court in 1977 struck down a New York law that prohibited the sale of nonprescription birth control to minors. The justices on the Court said that "the right to privacy in connection with decisions affecting procreation extends to minors as well as adults." In 1972, the Supreme Court decided that a law in Massachusetts that prohibited the sale of nonprescription birth control to unmarried persons was unconstitutional. There are no restrictions on minors obtaining nonprescription birth control.

The rights of minors to obtain prescription birth control, such as birth control pills and diaphragms, is not so straightforward. Federal law requires state public health services to provide birth control to anyone of childbearing age receiving federal aid, regardless of age or marital status. However, private doctors follow other rules. Some states allow doctors to prescribe birth control to minors without parental permission and without notifying the minor's parents. Other states allow only minors over a certain age to obtain prescription birth control without parental permission. In some states, that age is only twelve or fourteen, but in others it is sixteen or even eighteen.

Pregnancy

When a minor child or teenager becomes pregnant, she has most of the same rights that a pregnant adult has. First, a pregnant minor may seek medical treatment for pregnancy testing and prenatal care without the permission of her parents. The doctor providing the care has a duty to keep private the name of any minor seeking such medical treatment. The doctor is not required to notify the minor's parents or the father of the baby of the pregnancy or treatment given.

Minor girls and women have the right to terminate their pregnancies by abortion. This right is guaranteed to all women by the 1973 Supreme Court decision in *Roe v. Wade*. Whether minors must have parental permission or whether a doctor performing an abortion must notify the minor's parents of the planned abortion is not so clear. In 1976, the Supreme Court held that minors, just like adults, have a right to privacy in the decision to have an abortion and that the state could not give parents the authority to override a decision of their daughter to have an abortion. However, many states made laws that required doctors to notify the parents of a minor seeking an abortion under some circumstances.

In 1979, the Supreme Court decided that a state may require that a minor girl obtain a court order before having an abortion instead of obtaining parental permission. The Court allowed this only if the girl's identity was kept private by the court and the court provided the order quickly. Then, in 1981, the Supreme Court decided that states may make laws that require parents to be notified that their minor daughter is seeking an abortion if the minor is living with her parents, if the minor is dependent on them for support, if the minor does not claim to be mature enough to make a decision on her own, and if the minor offers no special reason why her parents should not be told.

A minor who claims to be mature enough to make the decision to have an abortion without parental permission, and who can show that there is a special reason for not notifying her parents, is entitled to go before a court to get an order

State laws determine when couples can marry. (Dennis Degman/Uniphoto)

exempting her from permission. While many states require parental notification before a minor girl can have an abortion, some states, because of court orders, do not enforce these laws. The law on a minor's right to an abortion without parental permission or notification is changing, and the Supreme Court will likely rule again on this issue.

A minor girl seeking an abortion does not need to have the permission of the father or notify the father of her baby that she is seeking an abortion. In most states, this is true even if the girl is married to the prospective father. Also, neither the boyfriend nor the husband nor the parents of a pregnant minor can force her to have an abortion if she does not want to have one. She can keep her baby after it is born or put the baby up for adoption. A minor has the right to give her baby up for adoption without her parents' consent. The consent of the baby's father may or may not be required.

Finally, a pregnant minor is not allowed to be excluded from public school. At one time, some schools did not allow pregnant students to continue their education or forced them to attend special classes or schools. Students who are pregnant have the right, under a 1972 federal law, to attend school and participate in extracurricular activities. Also, a school must treat absences because of pregnancy or delivery the same way as other excused absences.

Chapter Nine

People Who Made a Difference

Throughout history, many have fought for children's rights. In the early twentieth century, reformers began the fight by showing society that children were being exploited, abused, and neglected. During that period, Jacob Riis crusaded for the urban poor, exposing the extreme poverty of many children, and photographer Lewis W. Hine helped to reveal the poor working conditions of children when he photographed children laboring in mills and factories. Throughout the century, many children have fought for and won rights for themselves and other children. Mary Beth and John Tinker, Gerald Gault, and Dwight Lopez all changed the legal treatment of children by speaking up and complaining that they had been treated unfairly. Some lobbyists and lawmakers today fight for better protection and care of children in such areas as health care and education. Profiled in this chapter are a reformer, a teenager, and a lobbyist who have made a difference in how children are treated by society.

Jane Addams

Born in Cedarville, Illinois, on September 6, 1860, Jane Addams became one of the most famous and successful of the

Jane Addams (here in a portrait by George deForest Brush) led reforms of child labor practices in the late 1800's. (National Portrait Gallery/Smithsonian Instution)

social reformers. After graduating from Rockford Seminary in 1881, Addams traveled throughout Europe, seeking direction in her life. She observed the reform movement in England and eventually decided to establish a "settlement house" to serve the underprivileged in the United States. During this time, settlement houses were a major part of the reform movement: They offered cultural, educational, and recreational activities to the poor and disadvantaged immigrants living in the area.

In 1889, Addams and a college friend, Ellen Gates Starr, founded Hull House, which would become the most famous settlement house in the United States. Hull House was located in a crowded slum area of Chicago.

Many reformers lived at Hull House, including Julia Lathrop, who later became the first chief of the Children's Bureau. These people worked to improve education and housing and to make parks and playgrounds safer. Jane Addams and the others at Hull House also led the fight to end child labor.

The problem of child labor first came to Addams' attention during Christmas of 1889, when she offered some candy to several little girls at a Christmas party. The girls refused it, saying that they had worked in a candy factory and could not bear the sight of candy. Addams learned that the girls had been working in the factory from 7:00 A.M. until 9:00 P.M. and that they were exhausted. She began to learn more about the problem of child labor, visiting factories and other places where children worked. When a young boy was killed by a factory machine because the machine lacked a safety guard that would have cost the owners just a few dollars, Addams was horrified. She naturally expected the factory owners to feel the same way, but they showed no remorse and did not fix the machine. Addams began her fight for child labor laws, and she got Illinois to pass some of the first laws restricting work by children in factories. In her struggle for reform, however, she remained sensitive to the problems of immigrant families, who frequently survived only because their children worked.

In her later years, Addams became a pacifist and worked to end World War I. She founded the Women's International League for Peace and Freedom and sought to end the war through mediation. Although her views on the war caused many in the United States to dislike her, she eventually became one of the greatest women of her time. She wrote ten books and more than four hundred articles. Two of her books — *Twenty Years at Hull House* (1910) and *The Second Twenty Years at Hull House* (1930) — became famous. In 1931, Jane Addams and educator Nicholas Murray Butler shared the Nobel Peace Prize. Addams died in Chicago on May 21, 1935.

Walter Polovchak

Walter Polovchak was a twelve-year-old immigrant from the Ukraine when he challenged the legal presumption that parents' rights to custody and control of their children always take precedence over a child's desire not to move with his family. In 1980, after living in Chicago for six months, Walter's parents decided to move the family back to the Soviet Union. Walter wanted to stay in the United States, believing that his life in Chicago offered much more than his life in the Ukraine. He eventually became an American citizen after his parents returned to the Ukraine. While Walter lost most of his court battles, a federal court did finally agree with him that the welfare of the child must sometimes be weighed against the parents' rights to custody.

Walter was born in Sambir, a city in western Ukraine, on October 3, 1967. In describing his life in the Ukraine, Walter remembered long lines for food, bare shelves in the stores, political indoctrination in school, and punishment by his schoolteachers for attending church with his grandmother. The punishment he hated the most was being made to kneel in gravel on the classroom floor.

When Walter was twelve, his family was able to immigrate to the United States and settled in Chicago, where some of Walter's relatives lived. Walter loved living in the United States and was impressed with the abundance of food in Chicago's markets: "Aisles of food everywhere. . . . I found an aisle where they had nothing but food for dogs . . . and I remember thinking . . . 'The dogs eat better food here than some of the people in the Soviet Union.' " Walter's older cousin gave him a bicycle that he repaired, and Walter spent hours exploring his Chicago neighborhood on his bike.

Although Walter and his older sister Natalie adjusted to life in Chicago and began to enjoy it, Walter's father soon decided that life there was not as he had expected it to be and that the family was going to return home. Natalie told her parents that she was going to stay, and because she was seventeen years old, her parents told her that she could do what she wanted. However, when twelve-year-old Walter stated that he, too, wanted to remain in the United States, his parents forbade him to stay and told him that they would force him to return. In July of 1980, Walter and Natalie left their parents' apartment and moved in with their cousin.

A few days later, Walter's father called the police and reported that his son had run away. Walter was arrested. Because he did not speak English, he was confused and frightened at the police station, until an attorney, sent by his cousin, came to Walter's aid. Walter's attorney, Julian Kulas, was also an immigrant from the Ukraine. Walter told his attorney that he had run away from his parents "because I like it here. We waited so long to get out. [My father] said life would be different here, and it is. I definitely don't want to go back." Mr. Kulas was concerned because the courts seldom grant minors the right to leave home permanently if they do not want to live with their parents. However, he believed that he could show the court that Walter might be mistreated by

Soviet authorities for trying to stay in the United States. Then the court might allow Walter to stay.

Mr. Kulas and the other attorneys representing the children decided to apply to have them declared MINS (minors in need of supervision), which is the same thing as a PINS (person in need of supervision). Because the children had run away, the attorneys argued that they were "beyond the control of their parents" and that the state should take custody of them. The court agreed and eventually placed them with a foster family. The children visited their parents, and the court hoped that the parents and the children would eventually reconcile their differences. However, Walter and Natalie's parents — apparently distrustful of the legal system and tired of waiting — returned with their younger son to the Ukraine in August of 1981.

The American Civil Liberties Union (ACLU), which is usually a champion of children's rights, represented Walter's parents. The ACLU believed that custody had been taken from the parents unfairly, so it appealed the finding that Walter and Natalie were MINS. Eventually, the Illinois Supreme Court agreed that the juvenile court had made a mistake in taking the children from their parents' custody. The court believed that the children were not beyond the control of their parents; they had run away only once. The Illinois judge decided that the juvenile court had been influenced by the fact that the parents were returning to the Soviet Union; the children would not have been removed from custody if the parents had merely been moving to another U.S. city or state. The judge ordered Walter to be reunited with his parents. By this time, Natalie had turned eighteen and was no longer a minor, so this decision did not apply to her.

However, the Immigration and Naturalization Service (INS) had granted Walter "political asylum"; that is, the United States government allowed him to stay within its borders to protect him from possible political repression. The ACLU appealed this grant of asylum, because it interfered with the parents' right to custody of their child. Eventually, a federal court agreed that the INS had "all but negated a parent's right to bring up their children as Communists or Atheists." The appeals court upheld this ruling but stated that the parents' rights must be weighed against the threat to Walter if he were returned to the Soviet Union. A full trial on this issue was ordered. By the time this ruling was made, Walter was only three months from his eighteenth birthday, when he would be free of his parents' custody. Although Walter eventually lost all of the court battles and the courts upheld the parents' right to custody, he was able to become a United States citizen on October 8, 1985.

Walter's case is important in the fight for children's rights for two reasons. First, he challenged society's usual thinking that children must always move with their parents. Second, because of his case, a federal court agreed with Walter that the parents' rights to custody should not always be automatic but must sometimes be considered in light of the child's interests.

Marian Wright Edelman

Marian Wright Edelman is considered to be one of the greatest advocates for children in the United States. She is a powerful lobbyist who works to persuade Congress to improve and invest in the lives of children.

Edelman was born in 1939, to a family that encouraged service to the less fortunate. In 1964, after graduating from Spelman College in Atlanta and Yale Law School, she followed her family's lead and went to Jackson, Mississippi, to help the Civil Rights movement. She worked for the Legal Defense Fund of the National Association for the Advancement of Colored People (NAACP) and became the first black woman lawyer in Mississippi. She left Mississippi when she received a federal grant for a research project on services for the poor in Washington, D.C.

Marian Wright Edelman founded the Children's Defense Fund in 1973. (Children's Defense Fund)

When she was working on this project, Edelman began to study the needs of children, particularly poor children. Motivated by what she saw as the government's neglect of children and believing that children were a vulnerable political class, Edelman expanded her research project and founded the Children's Defense Fund (CDF) in 1973. As president of CDF, she advocates government services to improve children's health and welfare, to increase the amount of child care offered to poor children, to decrease the rate of child abuse, to prevent teenage pregnancy, and generally to improve the lives of children in the United States. CDF lobbies politicians to fund programs already in existence and to create new programs to address problems. Edelman and the CDF publish reports, editorials, articles, and newsletters to educate the public and the government about children's needs.

Edelman's greatest strengths are considered to be her persistence and her commitment to helping children. She is willing to be blunt in identifying a problem and forceful in motivating politicians to change it. Edelman is aggressive and unwilling to compromise on important issues. These qualities, combined with her use of data about the problems of children, have helped her and her advocacy group to improve the lives and rights of children.

Chapter Ten

Outlook for the Future

The rights of children have been changing since the first protective rights were made into law in the early twentieth century. Changes in societal attitudes have helped make these changes in children's rights. When reformers revealed the mistreatment of children in factories and mines and farms, for example, state legislatures and Congress began to pass laws against child labor. But it is one thing to make laws, and it is another to enforce them. Whether or not children's rights are enforced is often determined by public opinion. It was not until child labor was viewed as a problem that the laws requiring children to attend school began to be enforced.

Children's rights continue to change, and different trends in society today may well shape the rights of children in the future — and whether those rights will be preserved.

Privacy Rights

There may be changes in the amount of privacy students enjoy at school. While some states allow officials to search students' lockers, the privacy of students' purses and "persons" (including their pockets, clothes, and bodies) is currently protected. With increases in gang activity during the 1980's and 1990's, however, many children now bring guns and other weapons to school. By one estimate, as many as 90,000 students carry guns to class every day. School violence has increased: At least 65 students and 6 school employees were killed in school violence in the United States between 1986 and September, 1990. Another 201 students and employees were wounded and 242 were held hostage by students with weapons during that same period. This increase in violence at school will probably change the way officials and courts view students' rights to privacy on campus. For example, many schools are now using metal detectors to search for weapons as students enter the school building or yard.

Rights in the Justice System

Next, lawmakers may decide to make changes in the juvenile justice system, because many believe that this system is failing to discourage children from committing crimes. These people point to the growing number of children under the age of twelve who have committed serious crimes such as armed robbery and murder. Some children in inner-city areas participate in gang drive-by shootings. Children as young as nine are committing such violent crimes. Those who question the success of the juvenile court system blame the system's philosophy: They say that, because the goal of the juvenile justice system is rehabilitation, not punishment, children are not afraid of committing a crime.

Economic Strains

Changes in the economy during the 1980's and 1990's may also affect children's rights. During recessions and economic slowdowns, which the United States began to experience during this period, children's rights to proper care and to protection from abuse and neglect are not always a top priority. Adequate funding for programs that help such children

Young people can exercise their right to vote in the United States when they turn eighteen.
(Bob Daemmrich/Uniphoto)

becomes less likely. In 1990, people eighteen years of age and younger accounted for 40 percent of those who were considered poor. These children are receiving inadequate food, shelter, education, and medical care. Periods of economic distress also create greater pressures on everyone; as a result, the incidence of child abuse increases as families come under more stress.

The economy also plays a role in whether children are exploited at work. In 1990, during one three-day period in

March, Labor Department investigators found 11,000 violations of child labor laws throughout the United States. More than 80 percent of these violations involved children aged fourteen and fifteen, working in conditions that violated the Fair Labor Standards Act. These children were working during school hours, after 7:00 P.M., and too many hours per week. Many other violations involved teens aged sixteen and seventeen working in hazardous jobs: operating meat-slicing machines and paper-bailers, for example. One grocery store was employing children under the age of twelve, and many fast-food restaurants employed children who worked until 10:00 P.M. or in hazardous conditions. The Labor Department pointed to changes in the economy and in society for these widespread violations. It blamed a decrease in the number of sixteen- and seventeen-year-olds, so that employers were trying to attract younger teens. The Labor Department also cited an increase in the number of service jobs and a relatively low unemployment rate for adults as reasons for the increase in these problems.

Reproductive Rights

Finally, although children have the right to an abortion, this right may be changed as societal attitudes toward abortion change. While some groups support a minor girl's right to an abortion, other groups want to limit that right by pressing for strict parental notification rules or by prohibiting abortion completely.

This fight caused at least one fifteen-year-old girl to have her right to an abortion temporarily blocked by the Supreme Court. In May, 1989, a Florida girl identified as "T.W." asked a judge for permission to have an abortion. Florida law required that minors obtain parental or court permission to have an abortion. T.W. feared that her parents would abuse her if she asked them for permission, so she turned to a judge. The judge decided that the law requiring permission was "unconstitutionally vague" and struck down the law. However, the judge also appointed a lawyer to represent T.W.'s unborn child. That lawyer appealed the judge's ruling.

The Florida Supreme Court agreed to consider whether the law requiring permission was unconstitutional in the fall of that year, and granted T.W. and other minor girls the right to abortion until the law was considered. The lawyer for the unborn child appealed to the Supreme Court, and Justice Anthony Kennedy blocked the girl's right to an abortion. Later that week, the entire Supreme Court lifted Justice Kennedy's order and gave permission for the girl to have an abortion.

In the United States, as a result of the 1973 Supreme Court decision *Roe v. Wade*, the law is that women and girls have a right to abortion. In the future, however, minors such as T.W. may be caught in the crossfire between foes and advocates of abortion rights if judges decide to end their right to abortion.

An Ongoing Struggle

The threat of change in children's rights and the enforcement of children's rights is constant. To prevent negative changes and to ensure that their rights are improved and enforced, children and teenagers must know what their rights are, so that they will know when someone is taking advantage of them or treating them unfairly. Children and teenagers must also be aware of what is happening in their community, their state, and their country. What laws is Congress considering? What cases are before the Supreme Court? Such current events could result in changes in children's rights.

When children are aware of their rights and keep up on current events, they are better equipped to work against negative changes and for positive changes. Children can and should talk to parents, teachers, and community leaders to make them aware of problems. They should use all the resources that are available to them: agencies, hotlines, children's rights advocates, lawyers, the courts, parents, and school officials. Children and teens who learn about their rights are taking the first step toward protecting those rights.

Time Line

1869   Samuel Fletcher is rescued from his abusive parents in Illinois. The court fines his parents in one of the first decisions by a court that parents do not have total freedom in how they treat their children.

1870   Michigan establishes the first free public education system.

1872   The United States Supreme Court rules that government funds should be spent for high schools.

1874   Mary Ellen is rescued from her abusive parents in New York. The Society of the Prevention of Cruelty to Animals sues her parents and sends them to jail.

1875   The first agency to prevent abuse to children, the Society for the Prevention of Cruelty to Children, is founded in New York.

1899   Illinois creates the first separate criminal court system for juveniles.

1900   The child labor reform movement gains momentum as abuses of child workers become extreme.

1900   Approximately one-half of the states have compulsory education laws.

1912   The Children's Bureau is created.

1916   Congress passes the Keating-Owens Act in an effort to outlaw child labor abuses.

1918   The Supreme Court declares the Keating-Owens Act unconstitutional.

1918   Mississippi becomes the last state to make education compulsory.

1919   Congress passes a law taxing profits on goods made by child labor. The Supreme Court later declares it to be unconstitutional.

1924   An amendment to the Constitution allowing Congress to regulate child labor is proposed but fails to be ratified by the states.

1930   Most states have separate juvenile court systems or procedures by this time.

1938   Congress passes the Fair Labor Standards Act, prohibiting children under fourteen years of age from working, and regulating the work of minors over the age of fourteen.

1960's   Most schools end or modify dress regulations.

1967   The Supreme Court decides in *In re Gault* that Gerald Gault's arrest and prosecution violated his due process rights and that juveniles must be given protection similar to that given adults during arrest and prosecution.

1969   As a result of the Supreme Court's decision in *Tinker v. Des Moines Independent Community School District,* students are given First Amendment rights while in school.

1972   The Supreme Court strikes down a Massachusetts law prohibiting the sale of nonprescription birth control to unmarried people.

1973   In *Roe v. Wade*, the Supreme Court grants women, including minors, the right to have an abortion.

1974   *Goss v. Lopez* is decided by the Supreme Court, giving students due process rights in school when they face punishment such as suspension and expulsion.

1974   The Buckley Education Amendment (Family Educational Rights and Privacy Act) gives students and parents rights and control over student records.

1974   Federal law is passed prohibiting schools from excluding pregnant students.

1976   The Supreme Court holds that minors do not need parental permission to exercise their right to an abortion.

1977   The Supreme Court upholds the right of schools to use corporal punishment against students.

1977   The Court strikes down a New York law prohibiting the sale of nonprescription birth control to minors.

1981   The Supreme Court allows states to require parental permission in some circumstances where minors are seeking an abortion.

1981   The Court upholds the constitutionality of a California statute making statutory rape a crime only for males who have sex with minor females.

1989   Supreme Court Justice Anthony Kennedy blocks a Florida girl's right to an abortion after a lower court judge appoints an attorney to represent the unborn child.

1990   A nationwide three-day investigation by the Labor Department reveals widespread violations of child labor laws.

Publications

Atkinson, Linda. *Your Legal Rights*. New York: Franklin Watts, 1982. Atkinson covers a wide range of topics using fictional scenarios, some questions and answers, and charts. The discussion of young people's legal rights offers specific suggestions about how teenagers can check their rights with their own states.

Beaudry, Jo, and Lynne Ketchum. *Carla Goes to Court*. New York: Human Sciences Press, 1983. An excellent guide for students aged seven to thirteen, this is the story of Carla, who must go to court to testify after she has witnessed a burglary. Illustrated with photographs, the story explains what it means, and how it feels, to testify in court.

Benedict, Helen. *Safe, Strong, and Streetwise: Sexual Safety at Home, on the Street, on Dates, on the Job, at Parties, and More*. Boston: Little, Brown, 1987. This is an excellent reference for teenagers, aged thirteen and above. It is directed at teens who are becoming "sexual beings" and is intended to help them handle their new status and protect themselves. Included are sections on date rape and sexual responsibility.

Berry, Joy. *Every Kid's Guide to Laws That Relate to Parents and Children*; *Every Kid's Guide to Laws That Relate to School and Work*; *Every Kid's Guide to Laws That Relate to the Juvenile Justice System*; *Every Kid's Guide to Laws That Relate to Kids in the Community*. Chicago: Children's Press, 1987. These books, part of the Children's Press Living Skills series, introduce children ages seven to thirteen to their legal rights and responsibilities. The books use humor and colorful cartoons to illustrate different situations or questions that children may have.

Davis, Peter. *Fly Away Paul*. New York: Crown, 1974. A compelling, straightforward novel about a boy, Paul, living in an institutional setting — a modern Canadian home for boys aged twelve to sixteen. The novel describes Paul's rough life, his depression, the beatings he bears in the home, and his ultimate despair and decision to take action.

Guggenheim, Martin, and Alan Sussman. *The Rights of Young People*. New York: Bantam Books, 1985. A comprehensive guide for older teens. In a question-and-answer format, this book explores many issues, including rights at home, in school, and in court, as well as young people's social and political rights. Legal citations are included. The variety and depth of subjects covered make this an excellent resource.

Harrah, Michael. *First Offender*. New York: William Collins, 1980. This 186-page novel for children aged eleven to thirteen chronicles the inequities of the juvenile justice system. The story details the difficult life of the protagonist, who, although innocent of any crime, is locked up in a child detention center.

Haskins, Jim. *Your Rights, Past and Present: A Guide for Young People*. New York: Hawthorn Books, 1975. Haskins' thought-provoking survey of rights for older teens covers work, school, courts, and home, using case histories as illustrations. This book challenges society's assumption that children's protective rights are necessarily good.

Price, Janet R., Alan H. Levine, and Eve Cary. *The Rights of Students: The Basic ACLU Guide to a Student's Rights*. Carbondale: Southern Illinois University Press, 1988. The question-and-answer format of this detailed guide provides broad, in-depth coverage of all areas relating to students' rights at school. Considered, among other topics, are First Amendment rights, tracking, student records, testing, grading, and punishment. Appropriate for older students.

Stein, R. Conrad. *The Story of Child Labor Laws*. Chicago: Children's Press, 1984. Part of the Cornerstones of Freedom series, this volume is directed at younger middle school students. The book presents the problem of child labor in the early twentieth century and graphically describes it and its reform by using quotations from journalists, social workers, and reformers.

Terkel, Susan Neiburg, and Janice E. Rench. *Feeling Safe, Feeling Strong: How to Avoid Sexual Abuse and What to Do If It Happens to You*. Minneapolis: Lerner Publications, 1984. This discussion of personal rights is intended to help children between the ages of eight and thirteen to avoid sexual abuse. Presents fictional accounts of a variety of problems, including obscene phone calls, exhibitionism, pornography, rape, and incest.

Media Resources

Behind Closed Doors: Crisis at Home. New York: National Broadcasting Corporation. Distributed by Kidsrights, 3700 Progress Blvd., Mt. Dora, FL 32757, (800) 892-KIDS. This thirty-minute videotape for junior and senior high school students tells the stories of teens suffering sexual abuse and other problems at home. Considers why running away is not a good solution.

Broken Trust. Toronto, Ontario: Telemedia Publishing. Distributed by Canadian Living, P.O. Box 220, Oakville, Ontario, L6J 5A2, Canada, (416) 482-8600. This thirty-minute videotape teaches teenagers about the causes and effects of child abuse. Offers ideas on action to take if a child is abused.

Crimes Against Children: Failure of Foster Care. New York: American Broadcasting Corporation. Distributed by University of Oklahoma, attention Barbara Bonner, Norman, OK. This 1988 videotape investigates the status and problems of foster care in the United States.

The Child Witness. Distributed by Justice for Children, 720 Spadina Ave., Suite 105, Toronto, Ontario, Canada M⁵S 2T9. This video is designed for children aged eight through twelve who must testify in court. The thirteen-minute videotape explains giving evidence under oath.

Woman—Child. Distributed by Canadian Learning Company, 2229 Kingston Rd., Suite 203, Toronto, Ontario, Canada

M1N 1T8, (416) 265-3333. This fifteen-minute videotape considers teenage pregnancy, its causes and consequences. Frank discussions examine the responsibilities of the teenage father, the effects of pregnancy on schooling, and the health of babies born to teenage mothers.

Organizations
and
Hotlines

Child Abuse Hotline
(800) 422-4453 or (800) 4-A CHILD

This twenty-four-hour hotline is operated by Child Help USA and offers access to counseling for those suffering abuse. Personnel respond to those wanting to report abuse and can refer callers to agencies in their communities that can help. Callers can also receive information about abuse, including books and pamphlets listing abuse statistics.

Children's Defense Fund
122 C St. N.W.
Washington, DC 20001
(202) 628-8787

Founded in 1973 by Marian Wright Edelman, this is the premier advocacy group for children in the United States. Its publications cover subjects including adolescent pregnancy, child care, poverty, and education.

Clearinghouse on Child Abuse and Neglect Information
P.O. Box 1182
Washington, DC 20013
(800) FYI-3366; in District of Columbia, (703) 385-7565

Maintains and distributes information on child abuse and neglect.

National Center for Youth Law
114 Sansome St., Suite 900
San Francisco, CA 94014
(415) 543-3307

This group provides legal services, consultation, and information to children and youths needing representation. Their areas of interest include abuse and neglect proceedings, foster care, and children in institutions.

National Child Labor Committee
1501 Broadway, Suite 1111
New York, NY 10036
(212) 840-1801

This organization provides information about the rights of young people in the workplace, answering questions or referring callers to someone who can.

National Committee for Prevention of Child Abuse
332 S. Michigan Ave., Suite 1600
Chicago, IL 60604
(312) 663-3520

This organization provides information to children and teenagers about physical, sexual, and emotional abuse. Its publications are designed for children of all ages, including comic books to help younger children who are suffering abuse. For children in crisis situations needing immediate help, it will provide information about agencies in the child's community.

Planned Parenthood Federation of America
810 7th Ave.
New York, NY 10019
(212) 541-7800

Planned Parenthood provides information and educational materials on family planning and teen pregnancy. Local community Planned Parenthood clinics can assist teens with contraception or pregnancy services.

Runaway Switchboard
(800) 621-4000; in Illinois, (800) 621-3230

This twenty-four-hour hotline can help both young people who have run away from home and parents of runaways. Callers get information about shelters and other services.

United Nations Children's Fund (UNICEF)
Three United Nations Plaza
New York, NY 10017
(212) 326-7000

The branch of the United Nations that is focused on helping children of all nations. It can provide information about the state of children around the world.

INDEX